Roofs

By Stephen Sandy

Stresses in the Peaceable Kingdom
Roofs

Roofs *Stephen Sandy*

HOUGHTON MIFFLIN COMPANY BOSTON 1971

ISBN: 0–395–12719–x Hardbound
ISBN: 0–395–12720–3 Paperbound
Library of Congress Catalog Card Number: 71–159405
Printed in the United States of America

Many of the poems in this collection have previously appeared in vari-
ous publications, as follows: *The Atlantic Monthly,* "A Short Account
of the Japanese,"; *The Denver Quarterly,* "Tokyo Room" (under the
title "Japanese Room") and "Closing the House, Leaving the Country";
Harper's, "November Larches"; *The Harvard Bulletin,* "Charley";
Harvard Graduate Society Newsletter, "Charley"; *The New Yorker,*
"Mr. Reed of Martha's Vineyard"; *New York Times,* "Charley" (part
3); *The New York Times Anthology* (Macmillan, 1970), "Charley"
(part 3); *Poetry,* "Roofs," "Work," "Post Card, Moss Garden,"
"Suburb"; *Silo,* "Moving Out"; *The Vineyard Gazette,* "Mr. Reed of
Martha's Vineyard." "Kamakura," "Christmas," "January," "Local Con-
ditions," "Ginza Line," "Ancient Buddhas," "For Minoru Nishida,"
"The Two Lords of Maeda," "The Military," "Student Letter," "Where
I Was," "Sleep on the Floor," and "From the Fastest Train" appeared
in "Japanese Room" a pamphlet published by Hellcoal Press, Provi-
dence, 1969. "Moving Out" (under the title "Never Know") ap-
peared in "Mary Baldwin," a pamphlet published by Dolmen Press,
Dublin, 1962. "Home Again, Looking Around" was published in
broadside form by William Ferguson, Cambridge, Massachusetts, 1968.

Contents

Closing the House, Leaving the Country

I swing in
and a Barred Owl posted on a fence
meets my headlights;
gripped in the long, invading stare.

I switch off — and then
on, and watch
the bird dress in his great wings
and mount into a pine;

out of range, but keeping track.
It is September, I am going.
The windows are locked, the last storm
tightened in its slot.

I fill a basket with late grapes
and the first red leaves, for friends.
The pipes are drained, appliances hid
from vandals and hunters in the eaves.

And I have locked my valuables up
or given them to friends
for safe keeping
— or for keeps.

The field mice wait
in the hollows of late hay
uncut and frosted. The upland pasture
lies quiet under the quiet sky.

I let the car coast down the hill
getting one last glimpse

through the rear window.
It is empty. I do hope

everything is put away.
The moon will be down soon now,
and the mice will file inside
free from our possessing eyes.

Kamakura

As the flesh of a lemon
gone smoky, drained of sour,
the live flesh of the giant crayfish
to my eye — and tongue. Then

in the sea's sunlight we stand for photos,
taxi to the great bronze Buddha
"made out of the clean funds collected by the priest."
We step inside that deity to hear
our whispers, amplified, come back to us;

and find that on the pitted rib-cage cling
English words, "Hamilton, *Parthia*, 1890."

I see;   I see your lip
one corner yellow with yolk from breakfast.

Tokyo Room

When I moved in
by chance, on the table,
a dead *bonsai* stood,
efforts of careful
careful fingers halted.
Not care nor water
would any longer
aid those poised limbs

and I may not see you now
you come to mind only, and then
my flesh
aching as blood
gone crystal in the vein
from each
delicate
touch. You have become
your caresses

in me, yes,
as we drift onward
                    dead
only to each other.

Roofs

Sewn straw, exact pattern. Fields of rice-sprigs
evenly set, a mile of herringbone tweed.
The town, a sea of gunmetal, fish-scale tiles.

By morning each floor a casserole of pillows,
coverlets, comforters, towels: flown nests. Imprint
of bodies, fading. They fold the beds away,
the room waits empty all day.
                                                    All day the bodies
circle, leaving no impression on each
other. Tooled in the foundry of the streets.
School-caps, factory-packed subway, miracle train:
one territorial imperative,
an emperor's.
                        On his platform one yard square
perched on a roof that slopes in waves of tiles
up toward other tiled cascades, the karate student
for hours does running in place, deep knee bends
on his surfboard perch. All his free time to make
his body efficient, tight, exact, rising
and falling, mint piston pumping in its shaft.

The Bath

Small chunky feet and flat
stomachs. How different
my body is!
     An old man
chuckles at the size
of my feet. My white,
my rougher skin.
     Clearly I
am not Adonis,
never could have been
ever so fair.
     No, no more
than I will pass for
Japanese in here.
Down the misty
     hall they squat,
silent, or loll and
drop words in the pools.
They half watch each
     other, and
me. No leers. No side
show here. The gods had
their cerebral
     day. One big
childlike fellow smiles
at his fat belly,
twenty men scrub
     down before
mirrors, a tattooed
gang boy poses. Men
are not equal;
     bodies are.

Ikebana

Yes the lady tries
for bouquets to fit that vase.
She comes up here with
clippers and a saw, dragging
six feet of pine or bamboo

hacks at it hours
my floor a woodcutter's yard.
Then a few cherry
blossoms. Or a rose. A rose,
cherry blossoms. Or the rose.

In the end she goes
back to an easier shape.
The widemouthed and the
tall ones are too hard for her.
You remember the way you

went picking flowers
in the woods, lady-slippers
and columbine, ferns,
columbine and fern, lady-
slippers, every one:
     then, home

stuffed them into a
mason jar? Or not ugly
and not loved wedding
present? Which way is better,
easier, if any, on us?

November Larches

Maple and elm have done
  with their gold and their
    mulberry, yet

still this gleam comes, back, fur
  in the fogged windshield;
    passive;   passing.

This one wet golden gray
  they come up: a slow
    burn, nightlights low

in the dimmed house of frost.
  There is reason in
    remembering these

larches yellow, young, come spring:
  seeing how low they are
    turned for winter.

Christmas

Balancing
twelve bowls of hot soup, he
peddled into traffic.
Vanished in fog among
     ruby lights.

@

From the fields
this crowd has come to town.
Standing in line, it learns.
Bashfully we smile when
     the train rocks.

@

These mornings
the market is dead. You
hear hands clap, greengrocers
hoarse above their orange
     pyramids.

@

Drunk myself
I can't stop eyeing her.
Watching the young girl cry
because she wants to go
     with both men.

Keats and the Stem Christie

In from the slopes I sit among the Japanese
watching a science fiction on TV
with Death as Superman from Tokyo
when, after four days in these wind-wrung drifts,
I suddenly think: John Keats

the fine profile, almost the endless grit
to write on about Hyperion and the soul

— these young Japanese, during the ads,
stand up at a mirror nine feet wide
with easy joy in their human beauty
turning to see if ski togs gracefully cling,
running a finger down the outline of a face —

Superman limbo, this strange lingo,
my sixty-seconds for the desperate boy is up.

January

Quiet
on Tokyo's caterwauling back
of town Kitaku

as sun-
rise in undersea still haze
picks out the smog

again
yellow unequal *click* globed
clock of bleached

oak clogs
slapping the bar boy's bare
soles down empty

street tracks
the frozen winery closed
Mama-san boozed

asleep at the counter
Mama-san dreams prosperity
a fine cock

ox-tired
the wet boy doles *click-clocks* out
to trains saying *dawn*

outward
flower straggling up through deep
water to sun.

A Short Account of the Japanese

Still in step, arm in arm, the Japanese
   do nothing, not even
      skiing, alone.

Sailing them up like swallows the ski lift
   locked to one pace
      controls the spaces

between the bodies floating. Such a gift
   must have been invented
      by the Japanese!

Boys and girls wrapped carefully in sportive
   uniforms, like gifts strewn
      in the tinsel snow,

they plummet and traverse and do snowplow
   turns together, never
      falling and never

stepping from line: until at last they go —
   whoosh!   cartwheels — losing their
      balance together.

Prince Genji's Dance and Triumph

1

Could Genji, if he lived,
tell us what
Heian gentlemen did, beyond their doing it?
That Genji danced before the emperor
who wept to see such grace
while the sun set
beyond those pillared wavering sleeves,
such grace
as might remind the cloistered king
of sadness
deep as any bumpkin's
plodding his Grace's fields
slowly toward animal death. What man
might breathe so, so
thoughtlessly,
but to begin
again, as Genji, the different tempo?

What is your maple leaf that streams,
red tag of passing, ours,
that bolts toward seed, wind, the dead
harvest on bone-white stone,
this court?

2

Would they speak of such
wary abundance and stark
gentleness, surfeit
of self? And the familiar

stroke of sword? Can I know
in my own flagging
my own? The art to keep:
and what strange art is that
which only dallies and does not give,
a dust which grows on life?

How shall he kill
the part of him that kills?
Someone must make the gesture granting freedom.
May he come
raising his hand
sowing like sunlight after storm
freedom from fear
in the ruler's heart!

The sun falls in long shadows of the acacia saplings
across the field that fresh wind wimples.
Beyond the speed of light
warm across my hand
lies the void. We may not
kill what kills us. And such
knowledge is just bearable
to an emperor bearing all his pride,

man squeezing the planet from his life
as if to purify his chalky bones
of the rich waters of his soul.

Home

Sleet strings one streetlamp,
makes silver gongs of tiles. Dies
away. Past midnight
the lady across the street
still plucks her *koto*. Silence.

Dinner in Roppongi

Helpless as tied mice, three to a plate, warm squab;
and Rhine wine, behind pillars stuccoed to look
like pillows. Dinner in Roppongi, inside

"another world" where sliding screens are *something:*
"you've a real flavor of the Orient here . . ."
Though he admired the old Imari, priced it,

he launched his California smile at us
like a chiding finger. *"Lust,* remember,
has the same root as *luxury."* So lust

drives the drained body — scanned by so many
kamikaze eyes — lord now of our cool
table reflecting crystal and avid heads

to cruise for trinkets ("world travel," Ch'ing
porcelains, respect)? That bent to come alive
keeps;   the helpless need, need to arrive.

Local Conditions

The hills, adrift in mist, do move.
                              Reluctance
to speak hints knowledge of the road. This
maintenance of solitude — or the facsimile
of solitude.
                In this country you are always
within two miles of rural beauty spots.
Go there, stand among the bamboo's silken columns
to watch the pond, or in the thatched pavilion
avoid the April drizzle.
                        In two minutes
you hear breathing.
                    Other solicitors
of solitude stand hidden
behind green fans of rhododendron and long grass.
                              The crane looks up.
A cloud passes. Mosquitoes share you
with other bodies aping privacy.
The truck behind the hill like a beast of prey
climbs crashing against branches, grunting;
you turn around and there
                            the cherry trees blush,
a wife pours her husband another cup
under the branches;
                    the branches reach beyond them
weaving a net of white odor that screens
the huddled tipsy family from the sky's
far discipline, untemptable repose.

Work

Kneeling here, writing:
"rainy season" at a low
table. Legs tucked,
tingling;   fresh lilacs stuck down
a tub of soda water.

I came to hate my
books. But that was not needed
either. Hydrangeas
let their blue sky-patches out
easily, by any wall.

Ginza Line

To the sun
that bears cosmetics for a summer

the eye of the rose is a marmot
astonished at popularity
and coat so red

outside the subway car the concrete
                                    darkness
                                    swirls
eyes of the women upon
each other
never farther
beyond the window
oblong black scream reflecting her coiffure

You must see the world
in its special way
of wanting to be seen

          on thrones on
          wooden legs
          lame beggars ride

a spider crawling up the wall
not a large spider, a
spider
I would have "sent it to London"
last month
with the deceased goldfish
from the ghetto aquarium next door
     we (soused) flushed down

this morning I let him crawl along his way

Ancient Buddhas

Outside, the blossoms bend with purses of sky-blue,
now and then handkerchiefs white as a girl's arm
flutter from their open lips,

numerous lovers practice karate, strolling, dancing on the
walks,
a butterfly escapes from the young girl's bosom,
she brushes petals from her skirt and climbs into the museum.

Outside their glass windows
they watch a cinema of lovers passing
and one girl peering at their deft repose.

Unable to hold onto the heaviness glowing
inside their sloping shoulders and bent heads
the gilt flaking off their robes and arms

they stare on through darkness
dazed by its simplicity.

Poems for a Wind Bell
(to be written on strips of paper, tied to the clapper)

The low
music
it makes
combing
our hill
— will the
wind hear?

❦

No sense
swings here,
a wind
has no
ear for
the wind!

❦

The flock
sparrows
form and
keep to
flying
through five
power
lines does
not change

as this
bell winds
reach with
no change
and touch
unmoved:

exact
the song
dying.

❦

(Wind Bell,
keep me
from harm
when I
carry
you far
over
thousands
of miles
of sea
thousands
of feet
above,
to one
other
country!)

Kathmandu Faces

Mud and dust in the refugee
nursery yard. Tibetan babies

in blue loose-sewn cast-offs
of Pan Am hostesses.

He paws the plastic
strangeness of a little yacht

grips my legs tight;
unblinking eyes: *what are you?*

    the shaved, small skull
    smeared with purple salve.

        ➦

Eyes lowered, the bronze repose
of the bodhisattva, his face

ringed by a headdress of sockets
empty, nothing missed

where vandals pried
cabochon rubies from the halo.

    Moon craters;
    small-pox pits.

        ➦

The widow eating her husband's insurance
describes Mount Hood to the guide

who tried to show Ganesh-himal above
at the edge of her dark glasses;

snow thrones behind her head.
She saw a pony in the road

  on its side,
   legs stiff;   dead.

     ✱

In the sun
she holds

her own hermetic shield,
the rhinestoned handbag,

between her eyes and
kids that swarm her bright skirt,

  gritty squid, brown
  craning fingers.

Intersections

To begin with he loved this
jammed intersection of the present
this neon scrawl against cloud gleaming

as that concourse, distant and
unending, stars;   this laden crossing
of present and present, apartment

with deepest perspective, the
distance between mountain and mountain
flame and flame, soon slowly furnishing

one point, one hallowing space
of arms outreaching: and he embraced.
Whose bodies gathered light by touching.

@

Streaming below, away, back
the townsfolk and cornsilk countryside.
The sun dead ahead, not rising yet,
red coal in coral cloudbank . . .
Alaska. Then the mad hazard of
sparkles, Japan at random on black
air below.
                    A shy girl
her white American wedding gown
folded under the seat worried and
crammed, as for an exam,
thousands of miles for her groom's language —
and life — who met her down there;   drove her
to Hitachi City and
closed her with her oboe (she showed it

to me) and an in-law to teach her
proper tying of sashes.

I see you zoned on his matted floors
abandoned to a strict loving;   tied
to the pruned countryside and
factory siren. You practice your
oboe: the company symphony.

@

The caged squirrel spins his wheel.
The plumed rooster, stepping on his cage
as if plucking the metal threads, stands
where kamikaze taxis
scream cage-left;   cage-right, preoccupied
and uniformed, students press ahead.

And whatever the café
a tank glooms there, glass cell for fish, gold
carp and black;   sleek ghosts, diminished, of
forgotten geisha hovering
in the soft light of their floating world.
A film of fins, erotic silks, wafts

still water: bred thoroughly
in fantasy;   able to move, but
where, in such rooms? Their ancient nature
canceled slowly, need spun out
with care. The harmony that nature
so long attended, no longer here.

@

He slaps her freely — in dreams
— and probably she exercises
the same right when he has not behaved.

Mostly they love to discourse
with friends of their own sex. Silence may
be the deep conversation. Sometimes.

But if this so pure, wordless
exchange fails, then small talk (the smaller
the better) is pure delight for a

whole night. The sense of play, of
the whole trivia all stream upon;
that the spontaneous, *ludens,* keeps

always! Thus the sumptuous
useless strife with style, one lasting game
that all, engulfed by fashion, play.

For one night to be decked out
almost a Heian lady — almost —
is one thesis, one antithesis,

if mind is body, body
mind. So they play cards each night till two.
Ancient children, permission granted.

@

In Chiba-ken the eldest
son, at high school, made this of himself.

First among his fellows he excelled
as his father before him
in martial art;   the judo black belt.
Enticed to the temple precincts then

classmates in a band beat him.
The front teeth gold now, the father warned
do not resist. Elsewhere the winner
in running and in throwing
lies dead at the clenched hands of teammates;
chorus singing comment, holding hands.

                       @

No flies even in August
and at curbs now the frilled magenta
cabbage replaces summer flowers.

It is winter. As ever
Japanese flowers hustle the eye
but have no smell. On the packed corner

the vendor offers maroon
apples cantaloupe-size, and price;   what
a fine shoulder, that! At last I see

how this diminutive strives,
may be strong;   grown strong, capable of
heaviest burdens. We say *"History*

of Space Travel is well worth
reading." — 1776,
I think, and all that "strategy for

peace." Each semantic circus!
Each winner must turn in his trophy
on leaving the auditorium.

What use is it? Now even
apples are pollinated by hand
in the great orchards of Himeiji.

                    ◉

Or Mishima: "should these things
pertaining to spirituality
submit to the temporal? Once done

this can be an example
for others," wrote holy Becket. This
technology, the doom of Nippon.

                    ◉

Experts in adversity
you have looked hard, exacting too much
of nature. For example the branch

of a normal, blooming plum
you see not bunched, sun-reaching, aligned
with others, as in plums photographed

ever so artistically
in Trieste or California,
but as pruned, by hand in life, by mind

in eye, to zigzag so and
so: as if a painter or the pained
gullets undernourished for ages

by a short food supply and
a strict Bosatsu, decreed that this
world should not go scot-free;   and to keep

nature from making the mind
a monkey with the jitters, bind this
green world (of petals holding home wide,

straining to call bees through days),
feed it on discipline, and water.
So they teach, a cold dream is this world;

so this teaching would enjoin
man to mind Southern Paradise, a
jade mountain;   and saplings to favor

elegant disillusion.

@

Here, lying awake in this
fireless house I hear Ann now;   I
don't know where she lives, how far she comes.
She comes with winter sunrise,
the rumble of first commuter trains;
in the white smock and socks and slippers
forlorn she thrashes with our
mess, the dirty dishes and dirty

clothing. The household sleeps;   her noises
rouse me;   but they hold me, still.
We do not belong to ourselves;   even
the night soon belongs to a morning.

Mr. Reed of Martha's Vineyard

They found his kayak but they never found him
I thought for no reason sitting in Tokyo
                eating my shrimp rice and bean sprouts
watching the bulge of a five-months-pregnant woman
standing, waiting to get my seat.

Why do people I find myself asking
forget this needed thing — to be
generous to themselves?
                        You, Alex,
the carefully gardened, wind-combed hill,
I remember the ample light-swept spaces
of the clean house he built for himself up there,
who tossed for a week or so while he became
debris, strewing some floor of the Atlantic.
                It was winter, I think,
and he was a good swimmer.

The woman has found a seat. These Japanese
are so patient
                and expect so little, except good manners,
not comfort even.
                Alex loved shells and driftwood
and is dead, a lone gardener, and I
am sitting in Shinjuku, in Tokyo, thinking it over.

Peephole

Holding my breath
to see who this may be out in the hall
just sauntering to and fro
I wonder if this body came for me
appearing at first a giant
then a, pea
in the lens that embraces and distorts him so.
Holding my breath to see who this may be

I can't remember
that he cannot see me.
But does he know? How much does he know?
I wonder.

If this body came for me
with tiny head and feet that gingerly
prop up a body like a buffalo
why hold my breath?
To see who this may be I'm safe in here

the fool among us three,
myself, that stranger
and his imago.

I wonder if this body came for me before,
this trunk ballooning casually
keeping me up with such old tricks
this foe
holding my breath.

To see who this may be
I wonder, if this body came for me.

Post Card, Moss Garden

This might have been where Lady
Murasaki read

advantaged exile down from
court, "over the hill"

yet beautiful, read and read
and then lay buried.

Over these hills of moss lies
the age of Thirty

a tall white wall surmounted
by tiles incised "yin

yang" and by, beyond, green trees
waxing coherent

in blue skies, no obstacles.
You see distances

closely. Farther over land
than water. No obstacles.

For Minoru Nishida

Torn, yellowed and frayed, but still I saw
the shore like snowdrifts under cloud;   on the burred
horizon seen perhaps at thirty yards
in beach grass, screened to meet invasion, three
Japanese in uniform, battalion caps on straight.
One machine gun barrel nudges the sky
where sun through haze bursts like a small explosion
from the ready weapon: an old war snapshot
someone had sent to someone he had loved
in Niigata.
          The city, ramshackle, gray
sprawls like spare parts along a spongy delta
that melted snow pulls yearly from the mountains.

Willing to please, my host describes his town —
"the earthquake capital of the world." Ten-foot
photo murals show whole apartment houses
tipped on their sides like tumbled shoeboxes,
curtains hanging straight out from windows, chairs
and dishes piled at one side. Another mural:
the Premier congratulates three grinning soldiers
(they were digging in the sediment of homes):
stripped to the waist, sand stuck in sweat on muscles,
gleeful as romping children at the seaside.

Over the river, bridge ripped and sealed again
and again like an unhealing wound, I walked
pacing the silent, heat-slowed crowd. I paused
in a dark and bypassed shop where the patina
of a well-worn old oak box gleamed softly.
The ivory dowels held dovetailed joinings tight;
painfully wrought simplicity. I bought it

and carried it over the packed bridge to my
concrete hotel that listed, solid and heavy,
some ten degrees none would admit, all blows
and lurches of the earth canceled from mind.

In the box I found that snapshot from the war
and thought of you. Once you were a private
trudging Manchurian and Chinese hills.
Now you are a professor, precise and mild;
once you carried a gun by the Yellow River,
now you are an expert on Mark Twain.

The Two Lords of Maeda

Small pines tormented into exquisite
models of ceremonious behavior;
deep in a central grove of cryptomeria
behind a foot-thick wall, an inner garden,
and set in this a pleasant house with vast
verandas where cushioned floorboards wait
to groan warning when at night the intruder
seeks his advantage through sliding screens:
this is the place where the Lord of Maeda
puts the Lord of Maeda who precedes him.

Across a deep defile made deeper by a moat
rises the fortress of Kanazawa's Lord
under whose cedar portcullis bossed with steel
the Lord Emeritus may ride no more
subject as he may be, toothless but hungry,
to cozzening blandishments, courtly girls
of subtle men ambitious for estate.

No grandee now, the brush still sure in the hand
frail now upon the sword. Yet memoirs or
statements to the people by senile leaders
the Maeda held unwise;   as well, unsuitable
for an old man in a garden, called a sage.

The Military

"— Jim. Jim":
MacArthur to Lazarus. Then down to tea
from Noritake cups and hotel spoons.
Scrubbed Wainright, wobbling from ice, Manchurian
desolation. A tiger unwhelmed, speechless.
"Was he but pocked Corregidor?" he asked,
chipped into talk. His weight told the weight
of answering for the dead.
                    The White House had
a bomb. "Your picture is in *Time.* What guilt?"

To a sea of sun, Bull Halsey on the bridge,
warm steel decked out, the flagged *Missouri* preened:
it all was to belong to him, that moment;
grim MacArthur, Shigemitsu frail in striped
trousers, and Umezu, dangling his sword,
more proud and still more grim . . . A form
of disbelief swelled Wainright's eyes. Bataan,
the witness-bearer, the man. Victory
there died. The Supreme Commander sat writing
his name in fragments, sealing submission:
and the first pen to Wainright.
                    "How is it done?
That I could stand in judgment for surrender
I did deeds. My men, bodiless faces
called me to stomach the thick soup. With power
surprising these rimlands, burning the calm
Pacific, time has fled, gone on forever
up ahead." So mused the general, and saw
a defeated giant locked in Lilliput,
bowing from the waist to tiny captors.
Being answerable was but an inward

not an outward thing.
                    When he walked in
their talking, muted among positioned tables
capped with white, broke on the ark of him,
this pitted flesh caulking a stalk of bone.

He rose, casting his arms wide. "— Jim. Jim."

Who cried only, "General!" before he cried.

Student Letter

After the declaration by emperor
to stop the war
many people in Tokyo killed themselves,
for instance, in front of the imperial palace.
But few people knows those facts.

Hence you must teach me
where you got the news or what sort of book
gave you the fact that quite few people knows.
To know the fact of our nation's subjection
is not so comfortable
but the fact of many people's spontaneous death
gives me more complicated feelings.

In the matter of what William Gass said
I must describe my feelings. I went
to Nagasaki
on an educational trip four years ago.
I can recollect those serious moment
which was given by the beamed materials
in the memorial hall.

But most youth after the War
are indifferent to those
nightmares
because of our no experience. Surely,
I think, those barbarious conducts
shouldn't be forgiven or forgotten at all
and we must not close our eyes
to the rebombing
at any place
in this world.

In conclusion I may say that most people
except sufferers
or the like
will not have ill feelings toward your country
but they will reproach
the suffocative fact
in history.

Where were you when the World War II was over.
Please share your experience of the war with me.
I'm now interested in the wars concerned with Japan
for the past 100 years. If you tell me your reflections
I can suspect more seriously.
You have abandoned such cursed things as useless?
In that war 3 million people were killed
on the side of our nation, especially
three hundred thousand people by the A-bomb.
Over the war between the imperialism
and militarism America won a victory.
What does this word mean?

Where I Was

In the dining room, on father's map of the Pacific,
red pins like boils started
in the blue skirt of islands and
ascended from atoll shoulders
to the bell crown and the heart
called Tokyo.

Bataan, Guadalcanal, Kwajalein, Tarawa, Iwo,
Okinawa: I learned
the names. Red buttons bulged like cells
cancerous with flamethrown death;   then,
bright tacks where kamikaze
darts hit bull's-eyes.
One last pin, a gold star that a neighbor lacked heart to wear
blossomed that long August
like a sunflower yellow and
final, covering half of Honshu.

Fitted out with the pocked map
on V-J Day
we drove downtown in the white Buick convertible, top
down, mother and father,
grandma, my brother and sister.
Confetti clouds swelled with streamers,
shredded phone books, cherry bombs,
sparklers blazing,
littered our eyes. Grandma caught a spark on her skirt and
                                                              cried
shame upon a sailor
at the curb.
            On the way home we

stopped at the factory;   father
spoke with the night-shift cutter
to halt cuttings,
olive-drab laid inches thick. Until mother hailed him back
father rummaged in his
packed storeroom for the old patterns.
That was 1945;   then
no one dreamed of the new style,
Dior's *New Look.*

                    ❦

Details, colors came through later.
Boot camp . . .
Then the Navy played its dark
spectaculars
to cheer trainees between technicolor V-D films
and talks on tying knots:
bandy-legged men did the fifty
yard dash aflame from Tarawa's
caves, or fell like coconuts
from the singed palms.

Screen for a Radical Friend

FIRST PANEL

Two decades after, Bikini
grew livable again. It lapsed
through primordial silence
to real estate once more. Citizens from
another country
enter the silver transports, time machines,
and fly backward toward birth.

Only the crimson crabs, remembered
delicacy, staple food,
were missing. They would not
return, no place in the warm shallows,
hasty pre-fab ecology Washington rigged:
banana trees, coconut palms,
Long Island clams.

The sand looked whiter than before.
What were the strange metal housings for?
A grown man walks in tennis shoes
on pavement, waiting for crops.
His whole survival-kit was home.

SECOND

Into the random wildwood now
zig-zag dry-stone walls
gathered from their plowing:

Yankees in vests thrashed pairs of oxen,
addressed the rockbound land.

"Be fertile, we will grow you, be still.
Cornfields, groves of the tended grape."
And made loaves out of stones.

Hedge poplar, black cherry, jungle of broomsticks
for deer now, woodchuck, rabbit and bear.
In Petersham, Massachusetts, a field
lies open still, a truck
garden in a craggy jumble, granite shards,
tons of them, piled three yards high, eight wide;
an unproclaiming Stonehenge.

   THIRD

"You said you wanted to build us houses
and make us medicine lodges   I do
not want them

where the wind blew free there was nothing
to break the light of sun
I was born there

we have returned glad
but the new
food has changed us

as death
        stones
even after generations
well up to snag the plow

almanacs tell us
it is the stars pull up the rocks
skyward by night
          even as moons suck
at the heavy heart of the sea."

Charley

(*Minnesota, May 1945*
DMZ, September 1967)

I

In Tokyo our gallant boys
dance rock-and-roll, squint eyes
wary at standing easy. They leer and reel
on a springboard tip and then
jackknife toward the electronic noise . . .

And Charley, when Time Inc. said he said
the President had his head
wedged about Vietnam,
              burning for honor or — who knows?
the Action he had said —
             married the Marines.
He showered vows on those

who took his word who taught him
shoot it out and shout "Yes Sir Yes Sir!"
            and sent him out like napalm
obedient to any itchy finger.

I hope the fields of Minnesota gave perspective
when he moved out
             as to the starting line
on the command, *survive, survive.*

. . . our juiced doughboys feel their girls.

II

What
did I tell you
when we met
last and it

"after the leeches and the food"
on a break
in the rain
was already up with you, Charley?

Mouthing the big cigar
like a gangster at the wheel . . .

cigarette between thumb and finger
the way we all even in junior high
learned not to
your men watching in wonder

him tasting the strange
(turned officer so young)
foreign taste
that smoke: and all was dark
except what sparks
he scattered there, stubbing it out

What could we do for you

you hugging your knees

who taught you
to raise your voice?

III

No more the wide Mankato pearled with ice
            under blue January sky
your arm around the shoulder of the friend who ran faster
no more the long hours pad in hand composing
            reasons for your belief
a belief in fathers has no reason

no more the simple passion of going first
your hatless straightness, the struggle, the deep worry,
            the dark Africa of being alive in a country
            run by chiefs without tribes
no more of all that, only your
            brief beauty in many hearts
in a time when fathers bury their sons, and you
            surrounded, cut down
in a war you were fated never to see,
            blinded by love for all men.

Moving Out

You never know to what your knowing tends,
you know as the soldier knows what he must do
and move uncertainly to certain ends.

And at midnight what the turn you turn portends
in the dense alerted woods is lost from view.
You never know to what your knowing tends

and don't know what it is gives way, what bends,
when you writhe through passions you by chance pursue
and move uncertainly to certain ends

and fail to tell which shapes are your few friends
through all the benighted, ready retinue.
You never know to what your knowing tends

as the soldier does not know what he defends
when he moves out, nor does he wish to know,
and moves uncertainly to certain ends;

you lose the thread on which your life depends
and never hear the shot that rips you through;
you never know to what your knowing tends
and move uncertainly to certain ends.

Suburb

Are the rats little
Buddhas? Poisoned by the old
lady upstairs they
do not know it yet. And look
with their usual
cynical sweetness at us
from the kitchen floor.
Their tails still brush our *shoji*
at night. They still play.
They get used to everything.
The style of dying. Of us.

Sleep on the Floor

One cold March morning,
a tremor from the earth.
I start from sleep
and look about for the woman
who has shaken my shoulder.

In bare dawn outside
windless branches nod to the sun.

       ❧

At the bank a block off
the alarm cries   softly
folded between the billows of
a coastal storm.

Sleet-shouldered wind
hurls itself
against my walls
like surf. The building
trembles
acknowledging
more ways to go
than earthquakes.

The alarm brings no one.
Perhaps the owners in their beds
and whoever   must answer alarms

know in their hearts
it is only the burly wind
their bank cries to in fright.

Process

These cucumbers
might have come
from my own garden.

&

Friends with me
to the airport
to the last moment:
go with the departing at least
a part of the way.

&

On the train —
I could not rest my head
on your shoulder
if I knew you.

&

Moist cedar thatch
sprouts lichen and moss.
18 years: time
to re-do the roof;
and the model at hand.

&

Across this Tokyo
the taxi man
does not know my destination
until
he gets near it.

Shore

The stormbird
out, overhead,
circles in darkness. His ring
is inferred.

Up somewhere
out ahead
or behind this spit, lies his aim,
his need.

And gulls strain
on the sea-groin,
adze trawling their cries between stars
and white foam.

Their lone song
does, does belong
on this delta of the dark world.
All, they ring

out, they roam
pluming the stream
of wind, dervish of storm, shriven
of sensed doom.

I would know
how well they do
in the wheels they ride and the posts they keep,
here below.

From the Fastest Train

(Kyoto/Tokyo)

Each field is gone again

freak snow erasing boundaries
and still the same as yesterday
save a few edges softened here and there . . .

What is their endeavor that
helmeted argonauts
burning for days through frost-paned space
seek keener distances than these
to speculate upon?

After the smogged capital
to see the splendor that earth
snowbound
sunbound conveys

dazzling on the morrow when snows
sealed by night truck ruts, work track, ditch
and haystack
burn in the sun

giving the land seamless
identity, time with space, imagine
heaven that state
of final assurance locked in a trance of light like this
lone farmer carrying sticks of fuel
down snow drift toward his gate.

And
in a bright bay of space
rides the black ship of Schoolmen's sons

from which glassy astronauts
all weightless and aware
plunge spacecraft snowshoes down
to tiptoe
seedless fields, quicksand dust,

quicksilver the cloudless day
that recedes always before them
into the black sun strewn everywhere . . .

is it undisguised
erotic sighs
        or just some
mild grief, "wild surmise"
when these brief desperadoes of themselves

look up from sandwiches and watch their world
an opened orange on the shore of night?

Black speck caught in sheeted amber

the farmer cared always
never to answer
        bends to mend his gate
into the sun strewn everywhere
micas of Kansai noon lodged

in the warm blood of
        work to do
gate hinges rusty   blood
in fingers numb red bands
in agate, gristle

and broken bolt:
        to be done
— begun before
knowledge and not ever

        done.

Home Again, Looking Around

After-breakfast walk
on wet grass: I
remember the path, the hickory,
rock steps to creek — displaced now, shoved
randomly (man
or the weather).
Last night I was dreaming: Tokyo,
the bed shook, swayed
in earthquake.
              On
under green-tea maples the wild
hydrangeas held
balls of wet light
the whole way to the fall. A white
pine, an old one
but still green, felled
alive by streams
eating, rib-cage of roots mined clean.
A white stream forked
at the trunk, now
in both our ways,
the path a creekbed of fat logs.

Wild sweet pea has
taken over, thigh-deep, sealing
the trail beyond.
From a taut beech
the bark bubbles
out to heal the streak that lightning
branded, charging
the green landscape to find a ground.

Some Dedications

"Kamakura" is to Ken and Yoshie Ohashi

"Christmas," to Gordon

"A Short Account of the Japanese," to Tokiko Matsudaira

"Prince Genji's Dance and Triumph," to Masao

"Work," to Shozo Tokunaga

"Ginza Line," to Tom Hall

"Poems for a Windbell," to Koyo Okada

"Intersections," to Ginny

"Charley," to Carl and Dorothea

"Moving Out," to Yukiko

"Suburb," to Mrs. Nakamura

"Shore," to Alvin Feinman

"Home Again, Looking Around," to William Alfred